E220159616

CW01401498

Mountains

By John Wood

BookLife

©2018
Book Life
King's Lynn
Norfolk PE30 4LS

ISBN: 978-1-78637-135-5

Written by:
John Wood

Edited by:
Holly Duhig

Designed by:
Matt Rumbelow

A catalogue record for this book
is available from the British Library.

Photocredits: Abbreviations: l-left, r-right, b-bottom, t-top, c-centre, m-middle. Images are courtesy of Shutterstock.com. With thanks to Getty Images, Thinkstock Photo and iStockphoto. Covertr - Steve Boice, Covertm - Raimon Santacatalina, Covertl - Tom Reichner, Coverbl - Khoroshunova Olga, Coverbr - Warren Metcalf ,2 - Ruslan Gusev. 3: bg - Chaikom; br - Dudarev Mikhail. 4 - Vitalfoto. 5: tl - badahos; m - leungchopan; bl - dugdax; br - Willyam Bradberry. 6 - Vixit. 7 - celio messias silva. 8 - kavram. 9 - Anton_Ivanov. 10 - Raimon Santacatalina. 11 - Karel Bartik. 12 - dangdumrong. 13 - Khoroshunova Olga. 14 - Warren Metcalf. 15 - Brian Millenbach. 16 - Pavel Svoboda Photography. 17 - Pavel Svoboda Photography. 18 - Steve Boice. 19 - Julie Lubick. 20 - Victor Lauer. 21 - trekandshoot. 22 - Andywak. 23 - Tom Reichner.

CONTENTS

Words that look like **this** can be found in the glossary on page 24.

WHAT IS A
HABITAT?

A habitat is a place where an animal lives. It provides the animal with food, shelter and everything else it needs to survive.

There are lots of different habitats in the world. Each one is home to many different animals.

Mountains

Jungles

Forests

Oceans

MOUNTAINS?

Mountains are tall, rocky rises in the Earth. On very tall mountains, the **summit** is usually cold and covered in snow.

Mount Everest is the tallest mountain in the world.

When lots of mountains are together in a row, it is called a mountain range. Mountain ranges can be very long and some pass through many countries.

The Andes is the Earth's longest on-land mountain range.

MOUNTAIN HABITAT

Mountains are home to many different habitats. Lower down a mountain there can be forests and lakes. This is because it's warmer and there is more rainfall.

Mountain Forests

Higher up a mountain is the **tundra**. Only tough grass and mountain flowers grow in this habitat because it is too cold for trees.

Mountain Tundra

The tree line is the point where the trees stop growing.

GOLDEN EAGLES

Golden eagles are found in mountains all over the world. They usually make their nests high up in trees or on the side of cliffs.

A golden eagle's **wingspan** is around two metres. That's as wide as a car!

A golden eagle has claws on its feet called talons.

Golden eagles usually hunt rabbits. Sometimes they hunt bigger animals, like deer. They catch their prey by quickly diving from high in the sky.

GIANT PANDAS

Giant pandas live in forests which are high in the mountains of China. They like to live alone and avoid other pandas most of the time.

Giant pandas are very good at climbing trees.

A giant panda's diet is mostly made up of a plant called bamboo. Pandas often spend around 12 hours of their day eating.

Pandas eat a lot of bamboo.

COUGARS

Cougars live in the mountains of America. Cougars are also called mountain lions, panthers or pumas. These are all different names for the same animal.

Cougars mostly eat deer, but sometimes hunt smaller animals like foxes and mice. Cougars have strong **hind legs** which they use to jump a long way.

Cougars also spend most of their time alone.

ALPACAS

Alpacas come from the mountains of South America. Although alpacas live in the mountains, they are all owned by humans.

There are no wild alpacas.

A herd of
alpacas
grazing

When a group of alpacas live together, it is called a herd. They talk to each other by humming, and spit and shriek if they feel scared.

MOUNTAIN GOATS

Mountain goats live in North America. They have hooves that are soft in the middle, which make it easier to grip the small, rocky ledges.

Mountain goats going down a cliff

Mountain goats mostly eat grass. They live together in herds and stay safe from predators by moving quickly around the steep mountain cliffs.

DANGER

When harmful **gases** from cars, aeroplanes and factories are released into the air, they can trap heat in the Earth's atmosphere, making the planet hotter. This is called global warming and it is putting mountain animals in danger.

Global warming can make mountain habitats hotter. This makes it harder for animals to survive. When an animal is finding it hard to survive, it is said to be **endangered**.

SNOW LEOPARDS

Snow leopards live in the mountain tundra. They are endangered because global warming is causing their habitat to shrink, which means they have less space to find food.

AMERICAN PIKA

The American pika is also endangered. They also like to live in the cold mountain tundra but global warming is making it too hot for them to survive.

GLOSSARY

diet	things that an animal usually eats
endangered	when an animal is in danger of dying out
gases	air-like substances that move around freely
grazing	when animals eat grass
hind legs	back legs
predators	animals that hunt other animals
prey	animals that are hunted by other animals
shelter	protection from danger and harsh weather
summit	highest point of a mountain
tundra	a cold area where trees do not grow
wingspan	the distance between the tip of each wing when stretched out

Index

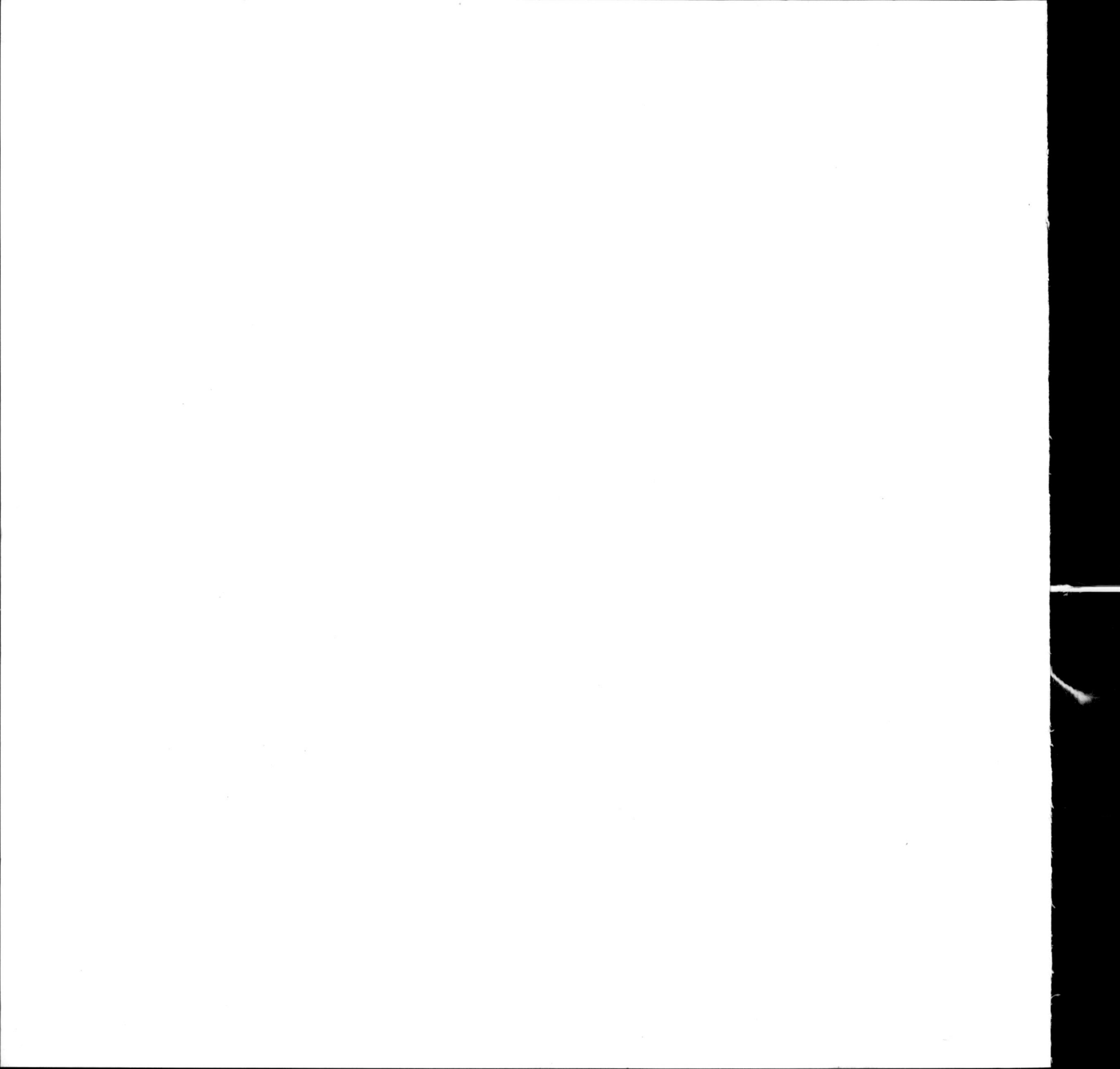